Tell You What!

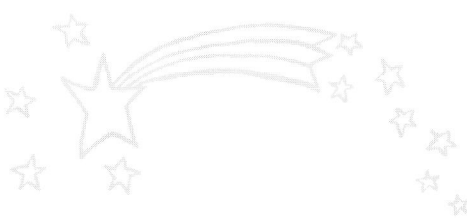

Foreword

by

Quentin Blake

CAMBRIDGE
UNIVERSITY PRESS

PUBLISHED BY THE PRESS SYNDICATE OF THE UNIVERSITY OF CAMBRIDGE
The Pitt Building, Trumpington Street, Cambridge, United Kingdom

CAMBRIDGE UNIVERSITY PRESS
The Edinburgh Building, Cambridge CB2 2RU, UK
40 West 20th Street, New York, NY 10011–4211, USA
10 Stamford Road, Oakleigh, VIC 3166, Australia
Ruiz de Alarcón 13, 28014 Madrid, Spain
Dock House, The Waterfront, Cape Town 8001, South Africa

http://www.cambridge.org

First published 2001

Printed in the United Kingdom at the University Press, Cambridge

Typeface Concorde *System* QuarkXpress®

A catalogue record for this book is available from the British Library

ISBN 0 521 00808 5 paperback

Contents

Foreword

by

Quentin Blake

I was delighted to be asked to write some words to introduce this book. I got even more delighted as I read the stories. You don't need to make allowances for them; they're real writing, by which I mean they are truthful, serious, observed, expressive, and they make us *feel* without being in the least sentimental – look at *A Message for my Brother*, for instance, or *Selling my Grandmother's House*. There are plenty of grown-up writers who can't do as well as that. And it's an art within the reach of all of us if we have a mind to try. You need a pencil, some paper and an imagination.

Thank goodness for reading and writing.

Quentin Blake

London, 2001

Introduction

The Competition

The Cambridge Young Writers Award was launched in January 1999 in the National Year of Reading, as a joint initiative by Cambridge University and Cambridge University Press. The competition is run through schools and is open to all UK children from Year 2 to Year 6.

Children are asked to write about something which has really happened to them and which is memorable to them, for whatever reason, whether it is a trivial incident or a momentous event in their lives.

In the inaugural year, we had a wonderful response and 25 winning stories were selected to appear in an anthology, *I'm Telling You!* which was published in early 2000. This year, the response has been even greater and the entries have poured in from children all over Britain so it has been even harder to select winners from so many pieces of such high quality.

David Blunkett, MP, who was then Secretary of State for Education and Employment, came to Cambridge to present the prizes in 1999 and this year Michael Morpurgo, MBE, the well-known children's writer, was the presenter. Here is what he said about the winning stories in *Tell You What!*

"For most of these exceptional young writers, this may be their first adventure into print. Wonderful for them and equally wonderful for us, their readers, to be able to enjoy their work. It is a real delight for me to witness the blossoming of this early literary talent."

The Judges

The 2001 final judging panel was chaired by Professor Dame Gillian Beer, former Chair of The Booker Prize judges; the other judges were Julia Eccleshare, Children's Books Editor of *The Guardian*, Jackie Kay, prize-winning children's poet, and Tony Bradman and Richard Brown, both children's authors.

Royalties

All royalties from the sale of *Tell You What!* will be donated to The Children's Society.

To Find out More

To find out more about the Cambridge Young Writers Award, contact me on 01799 531192 or email me: r.hayes@btinternet.com

Rosemary Hayes, Project Manager,
Cambridge Young Writers Award

Cambridge 2001

An Aurora Adventure

"HOORAY!"

I was overjoyed and excited when I found out that me, Mum, Dad and my sister Mary were all going to the amethyst mine that night (amethyst is a purple stone or gem). We were staying in a log cabin in the Finnish part of Lapland, near Sweden and Norway, when Mum told us the exciting news. But little did we know what else would happen.

That night we took our ski goggles for the long journey and set off on foot to the snowmobiles where we found a sledge towed by a snowmobile and prepared for a very bumpy ride.

"Here we go again," I thought. I had been on a bumpy ride before.

As we set off, thud!

"What was that?"

We went right up the huge ramp onto the path.

"Watch out, a big dip!"

Too late, bump! We were entering the forest, but it was still really bumpy and we were all huddled up trying to keep warm. Despite the magical snow-covered scenery, the wind was icy and the frost biting cold. Suddenly the lights went off and the noise died down. We had stopped on top of a mountain.

The next thing I knew we were walking off to the amethyst mine. First we were divided into groups, about three families in each. My group went to a small wooden hut to get warm while the other groups went to the mine. There were lots of chunks of gemstone on some wooden shelves in the cabin, but soon we were out of there and we trudged through the snow to the mine. When we got there it was half the size of the small cabin, but that was just the top of the stairs. The actual mine was much bigger but it was a long way down.

When we finally reached the bottom we were given a mini pick each, then we started hacking away at the rock. Each time you hit a piece of gemstone, sparks of blue flew from the pick. Suddenly, crack! A small chunk of dark purple amethyst came free. Full of delight, I showed it to Mum and Dad. But sadly as soon as it started it was over and we were walking up the winding steps with a piece of gem each.

Then we were out in the cold walking over to another log cabin where a man, a fascinating bloke who showed us pictures and told us about the Northern Lights, was sitting.
I liked the way he explained how the Aurora Borealis was formed, coming in all shapes and colours. The more he spoke about it, the more excited I became.

When we left that hut and went outside again I turned round and THERE IT WAS! The Aurora Borealis I had waited to see. It was bulging and changing shape all the time and luckily I know how it was formed.

Should I tell you? YES.

Okay. Well, some tiny particles from the sun's rays, which are

called protons and electrons, hit the earth's magnetic field and begin to glow. You would need a clear sky to see them though and I was lucky.

Back to the story. We all looked at it in amazement – I couldn't take my eyes off it. But we had to leave and return through the forest, winding our way back down through the cold, still trying to catch a last glimpse of the Northern Lights and at last to a welcoming fire back in our log cabins. I was tired but too excited to sleep but when I eventually did drift off, I still had all the memories in my head.

By David Whittle, aged 8
Whitechapel Primary School, Preston

Winner, Years 2/3 ✳

My Wish

My name is Sophie, I am six years old. I go to St John's School in Crossens. I think my school is the best! We do lots of fun things and we have lots of after-school clubs. My hobbies out of school are swimming and dancing. When I was little I really, really wanted a baby sister and when people used to ask me what I wanted for my birthday or Christmas I would always ask for a baby sister. My mum always used to get me a doll and so would Father Christmas.

I wasn't sure where you got baby sisters from but I knew you could get them from somewhere because other people I knew had babies. I was so excited when my mummy and daddy told me that we were going to have a baby. I felt it would take a million years for it to be born. When my mummy's tummy got bigger I sometimes went to the hospital to watch my mummy have a scan to see which it was going to be, a boy baby or a girl baby, but every time we went it was always in the wrong place so we couldn't see.

One day my childminder, Cathy, took me to the Botanic Gardens. I had been to the park lots of times before but I had never been to the bit Cathy took me to. It was a magic part of a special green house and right at the very back was a wishing well. Cathy gave me a coin to throw in for the fairies and said "make a wish". I wished with all my heart for a baby sister.

When it got nearly time for the baby to be born, my mummy made me a countdown calendar and each day we crossed off a date and every day it got nearer and nearer. We still had days left on the calendar when one day my daddy picked me up from school and told me that the baby was born and we went straight to the hospital to see the baby.

It had been born early and guess what it was?

A girl!

By Sophie Marsh, aged 6
St John's Primary School, Southport

A New Life in England

I was born in Gjakova in 1989. When we were in Kosovo we knew that the Serbian Army was going to attack us because we were told that Kosovo had gold under the earth and that it still has gold now. My family and the other people in the village just got away as best we could; we walked over the mountains without shoes and socks and only wearing pyjamas. We walked for six weeks like that. Every night we slept in the open air while some of the men kept guard over everyone. Some nights it was very cold because not everyone had a blanket. After six weeks we arrived at the camp in Albania.

I don't remember so much about the camp, but I can tell you some of it. First the camp had lots of tents made of canvas, like an army camp. Each family had a tent. Inside our tent there was one cooker, one carpet and three beds – one for my mum, my brother and me. We stayed in the camp for six months and we made some friends there. My dad came with us to the camp and went away for about four hours. He came back and then he said to my mum, "Take this money and look after yourselves. Buy something for Blauden and Bernard. Goodbye, we will meet again sometime together." And he went to help our people.

I often thought about what my life had been like in Kosovo.

I went to school in Gjakova when I was five. My school was so beautiful. It had clever pupils, and big rules. Nobody used to break the rules, even a teacher. The teachers knew me as a clever boy and they liked me. First we learnt how to add up and then we started to learn times tables 1 to 10. After the times tables we learned how to divide. In school we could choose what we wanted to play. I always chose football. I played with my friends and sometimes we played against other schools. We had one match against Year 3 and we won.

When my family left Kosovo we went on a train and we saw dead people who had been massacred. We left, my mum, my brother and me, because we wanted to live a new clear life but we left behind some people that wanted to stay and fight for our country. When I left I thought I will never see my country again, where I was born and where my friends are, and where I want to die.

One day I heard the news from the television: "In Kosovo, the Serbian Army went last night in Gjakova and there were many dead bodies found in the streets."

We really looked forward to going to London. We heard that Tony Blair allows the people of Kosovo to come to London. We had some money and we paid a man to take us there. We went on a train and stopped in some places and slept in an underground station. We went on another train and we came to London, at Waterloo.

We went to different places and saw lots of people. I was very sick and they gave me medicines for my cough and after two weeks I was fine. Then we got a flat and I went to my school, Hungerford Primary School, with my mum and my brother. Elaine, the secretary, said, "Have a seat please, someone is coming to help you." After a few minutes Kathie Walsh came and explained everything to us and we filled in two forms and we had a look around the school and found out about it and met our teachers. We did not start school that day but Kathie gave us some books to help us learn something.

We started school the next Monday and I was very happy. In London I found the clear life I was looking for, for ages, and it was exactly what I wanted. My teacher was Terry Hogan. He teaches Year 5 and he always looked after me. When I asked him to help me he did and gave me a dictionary in Albanian and English and that helped me so much to learn English. I also learned a lot of language with my friends as well as in class. I always learned all the spellings every week and got them nearly all right. I learned so much and finished Year 5 very well. We had six weeks' holiday and then I came into Year 6, into Miss Bolton's class. We have harder work and harder spellings but my teacher says I am doing well. I am really working very hard and I think I will soon be going to work with a higher reading and writing group.

I can tell you this, that I have really found the peace that I was looking for everywhere. I can't go back to my country because it is not safe and many of my friends died. When they were playing a bomb exploded. It had been placed under the ground. So I cannot go to my country until it is safe and peaceful again.

By Blauden Mustafa, aged 11
Hungerford Primary School, London

How I Developed and Lost an Allergy

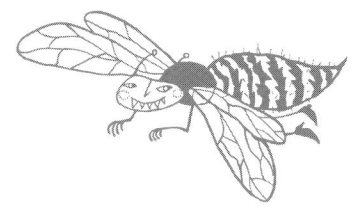

"Ouch!" I exclaimed.

I was playing football with my friends when Tristan kicked the ball into a bush. I was reluctant to go in as I saw a low-hanging wasp nest nearby. But then I saw a bull terrier charging at me like a speeding rocket, obviously wanting the ball. I rushed in and got the ball, making a swift exit. Then I saw a white streak fly past me like a javelin and knock the wasps' nest off the branch. A loud buzzing sound filled the air, with the terrier's high-pitched yips and its owner trying to call it in the background.

The swarm had the dog in hot pursuit, all except one rogue wasp who made a beeline for me. My friends were some distance away; I zipped off towards them. "Ouch!" I exclaimed. The wasp had injected its poison. I told my friends I had to go home. They went on playing football in a different place while I made my agonised way back.

At home I explained to my mother what had happened. She was very sympathetic and said that if I just left it, it would be better the next morning, with that reassuring tone mothers happen to possess. I took her word for it for an hour, when a sudden pain shot up my arm. Not so confident now, I went to my father; he was slightly more worried, but again I got the advice, "Sleep on it." What I wasn't expecting was "If it isn't better tomorrow, your mother will take you to hospital." In the end I did sleep on it, but when I woke up I was not greeted by my mother, but by a burning pain channelling through my arm. I got dressed and my mum took me to the hospital. The ten-minute car journey felt like ten hours.

When I entered the hospital a sanitary smell greeted me. We stepped into Minor Injuries after consulting a nurse. The twenty minutes until "Next!" was shouted out were a living hell. A searing pain kept on making itself present in my arm. We stepped into a room with a nurse in it. She had a rather neutral expression on her face but it was clear that she knew what she was doing. She observed my hand for a minute while my mother peered on anxiously. She said without warning, "I'm going to take a blood test, hold still." With that, she gripped my arm like a vice and plunged the needle in. Since then I have hated vaccinations. It hurt even more than the initial wasp sting! In an unworried tone she said, "I think you have an allergy." My mother gave a shocked gasp. The nurse then drew round the swelling with a black felt tip. "Go to Ward Three," she said. "The blood test will show in two days." She flashed me a quick smile.

In Ward Three I saw many children who seemed about my age. Over their beds were signs saying who they were and what ailment they had. A nurse directed me to a corner. "This is your bed," she muttered. It was quite close to the TV so I didn't mind. I talked to the boy opposite me. His name was Robert and he had sickle cell anaemia. I took an immediate liking to him. I asked him to turn the TV on as he had the remote. To my surprise Princess Diana had died the previous night. It was the talk of the hospital. On television I saw many young children laying down flowers and prized possessions. What happened to them, I don't know. A nurse then approached me with a small, sharp object. "No, no wait, you must be kidding … Yowww!" My scream of pain echoed through the building. "Enjoy your drip," she said, walking off. I was cursing under my breath.

Overnight a brave little girl called Rosy arrived. I forget her ailment but I shall never forget her. She was so brave. Neither of her parents were there and she was only three years old. I approached her and she greeted me. That day flew as I played with her and kept her company while also introducing her to Robert. When it was finally bedtime I couldn't sleep. My arm was in a special cast. Going upwards.

The third day was hard. First I had to have a bath with my drip and cable, then I had to go to school. Luckily, it was hospital school, it was easy. There was one good thing; I had been stung on my writing hand! I felt sick after school though; I had seen a pickled human heart! On return to the ward I realised one thing… I was the only Ward Three person to have to go to school. I made a mental note to have a chat with the doctor.

The fourth day was promising. The doctor withdrew me from school, I was off the drip and, best of all, I was going home the next day! Maybe I shouted a little loudly, but what the heck, I was going soon! My nanny brought my Game Boy. Everybody in the ward had a go, including the doctor, but I couldn't resist giving Robert sneak extra goes. The hours passed like a leaf floating, slow and happy.

I was finally leaving! I was dancing with joy! But then I saw Robert's sad face. "Goodbye Robert, I'll miss you." He just nodded in response. Rosy was crying into her pillow. I gave her a soft farewell before telling the whole ward goodbye. My mother then grasped my hand and took me out. It brought tears to my eyes then; it still can now.

That was four years ago. A blood test shows I've lost the allergy. I wonder where Rosy and Robert are now, from the four years that passed so quickly.

By William Lehmann, aged 11
Colet Court, London

The Fox

Though my bed was warm, I shivered as I got in. I was sleeping at my Grandma's house in the conservatory because the bedroom was being decorated. I couldn't get to sleep because in the darkness of the night I could see some shadows moving. I tossed and turned. Finally, after what seemed like hours, I drifted off.

Suddenly, I woke up. All around me were creepy noises. I looked out of the window and there, coming out of the trees, I could see a shadow. As it got closer I could see it was a big brown fox! As the fox came towards me it was leaving enormous footprints behind. I felt like I was in a dream and I was very scared. I thought it was going to get me because I was surrounded by glass.

I tried to scream but nothing came. I tried and tried but still nothing. I then tried to forget about it, but I just couldn't. I looked back up, then it spotted me! It turned around and ran. My heart was racing and my body was stiff. I looked out again to see if the fox was still there.

Thank goodness, it had gone. The garden felt deserted without the fox. Slowly I got back to sleep.

When I woke up I told my Grandma about the fox. She said it was just a nightmare. But when I looked out of the window I could still see the outlines of the fox's footprints.

By Alison Martyn, aged 10
Downsbrook Middle School, Worthing

A Frightful Night

I was on my way home from visiting Matthew (my friend) when suddenly a man came out from nowhere; it seemed that he never took his eyes off me. I was terrified! I could not move.

I thought I was doomed!

But suddenly I could move; I ran for my life (well that's what I thought anyway) but it seemed that my house was running away!

"Come back!" I shouted. Then I managed to catch it up and jumped right into my home. I never did see the man again.

I told my mum the whole story, so the only people that know are you, Mum and me.

By Bradley Price, aged 9
John Paxton School, Sawston

A Message for my Brother

Leosha, we have not seen each other since I was one and a half and you were three years older. I am now ten. I have seen you in photographs and that is how I remember what you look like. My life has changed so much since I saw you last. I have been adopted and I now live in England. It is very far away from Russia and you. This makes me sad and I cried because I miss you. But I love Mum and she loves me. I am happy because she makes me happy and keeps me safe. I don't have any nightmares any more.

I know that you are in the orphanage in Gatchina. I remember it was white and dull and cold. There were no bright colours and no lights in our bedrooms. There was no garden outside the orphanage for us to play in so we had to play inside because it was too cold. There was no television or radio but we played games. My best friend Vanya and I used to dance; Vanya left the orphanage before me. This made me sad and I missed him very much. Sometimes I was lonely even though there were lots of people around me.

The lady who looked after us had a round face and brown hair. She never hugged or kissed us. My favourite day at the orphanage was bath day. We travelled to a bath house by bus where we waited in a lovely steamy room for our turn. There was a big basin of hot water with a stool in the middle of it. We would sit on the stool and be washed by a lady who was rough with the wash cloth. It felt good to be clean. I am clean now and always have clean clothes to wear.

I met my adoptive mum when I was in the Children's Regional Hospital in St Petersburg. I was four years old and was having an operation on my mouth. The charity, which my mum set up, 'Sterling Work for Russian Children', paid for Dr Mercer to come to Russia to operate on children like me. He made me feel so much better. I came to England for another operation and stayed with my mum. I never went back to Russia. I was so scared of Mum's cats. I am still afraid of dogs but I love the cats now. Their names are Louisa, Felicity and Igor. They are so soft and warm.

I go to school at The Arts Educational School. I have had to work very hard to learn to speak English. I know you will not be able to understand this story because you can only speak Russian. But when I grow up I will find a way to tell you my story. My favourite subjects are maths, art and dancing. I have a book called 'The Famous Five'. It is very good to read and I love it.

My biggest wish is for you to visit me in London. My mum and I would show you all the sights. You could meet the cats, join me at school, eat chocolate biscuits and meet all my friends. But most of all I wish you could be adopted as well so you too could have a mum to love as I do.

Anastasia Kovaliova, aged 10
The Arts Educational School, London

Winner, Year 5 ✳

Blackberry and Apple Crumble

One autumn day my mum and dad said they would take me out somewhere. They said it was just a short walk to get there but I thought it seemed like ages. We walked along the old railway line. The tracks aren't there any more which is a good thing really. We picked loads of blackberries and put them in our bags. Dad said we were going to make a blackberry and apple crumble for pudding after our Sunday dinner. The only problem was, we couldn't find any apples.

Then my dad saw some apples high up in a tree. We couldn't reach them, so my dad threw a stick up to try to knock them down. We all had to stand a long way back so the stick wouldn't hit us when it was falling. He kept throwing the stick up and running away like crazy. When some other people came along we had to look busy picking blackberries again because my dad looked very silly throwing a stick up and running away all the time. I wanted to carry on walking along the railway track, but my dad was still trying hard to get some apples. Eventually one came down. It was a bit mouldy but Dad seemed very pleased with it so we put it in the bag. At the end of the walk we ended up with four carrier bags full of blackberries but only one apple.

I thought the next part of the day was going to be really

exciting. Dad said he was going to take us bowling because we were worn out with walking. When we got there they didn't have any lanes with bumpers, so we had to pick a lane without them. We typed our names into the machine but the machine didn't work so Dad had to call the man over to sort it out. We had to keep rolling the ball down until eventually we could start

our game. My brother went first and he missed all the skittles because the ball went down the side. It is quite difficult to do bowling with no bumpers. There weren't any lighter balls that they usually have, so I had to try a number 12. It was heavier than the lighter one but I managed to bowl with it and I knocked down most of the skittles on my first go. The final results were: 1st – my dad, 2nd – my brother, 3rd – my mum. I came last.

When we got home it was time to make blackberry and apple crumble. I helped make the crumble which is quite easy when you know what you are doing. Dad cooked the blackberries and the apple. There were quite a lot of blackberries so we had to put some in a bag in the freezer for another time. We had to wait for 30 minutes while it was cooking and it smelt really delicious. I was looking forward to tasting some at dinnertime. We had a big bowlful each but it was like crunching on a load of seeds and it tasted absolutely disgusting. I couldn't get the taste out of my mouth for ages. Next time I think we should have less blackberries and we should buy some apples instead.

By Edward Graham, aged 9
Dunmow Junior School, Great Dunmow

You Never Knew

Looking back, my earliest memory of my grandmother would be her answering the door and giving me a whiskery kiss after telling my sister Verity and I that we would break her doorbell. She does not even have a doorbell to be rung any more.

I never asked (Mummy would not be able to bear it) but I do suspect her illness had something to do with Grandad's addiction to sugar. You see when Grandma was young she had another terrible disease and when the doctors cured her they told her that if she ever ate sugar again she would become very ill. Even when she was well she would put Grandad's sugary things on her food by mistake.

Grandma has something wrong with her brain. She is in a Home and I have not seen her for over a year. Mummy does not want me to so I doubt I shall ever see her again.

I was only about four when Grandma began to forget things. By the time I was seven she was scolding us and wandering around asking us whether we asked for a comb when we did not want anything. I was too young to understand but it still upset me.

About a year later they moved away from Southampton, from the house where my mother was born, the house which I had grown to know and love, to a small bungalow in Trowbridge which was across the road from my Uncle David's house. The last time we saw them, before they left Southampton, Mummy advised me to take the cuddly toys I kept there home, as Uncle David was going to do the packing and might throw them away. By this time Grandma was putting things in very strange places indeed. She had managed to lose her bee brooch which before then she had worn every day. I think she must have put my patchwork dog somewhere like behind her dressing table by mistake because, when I took Tigger home, my darling Patchy was not to be found. I expect Uncle David did throw him away but he had no right to! Patchwork Dog was made for me by a friend of Grandma's when I was very little, to keep in Southampton.

I very much miss their old house but it would not be the same without Grandma. I can picture their bedroom exactly. You went into it through a door onto the landing. To your left was Grandad's chest of drawers and round the corner, the sink. Their toothbrushes were very old and in need of replacing, but familiar. There was also Grandad's old-fashioned wooden shaving equipment. Next to the sink there was the wide double bed made of dark wood with a cream bedspread. It was beneath this on the left-hand side where Grandma kept her 'biccies' in a large biscuit tin with a vase of flowers against a dark background on it. She would offer us a 'biccie' when we came in in the morning. Beside the bed was her medicine cabinet and across the corner was her dressing table.

I loved that dressing table, it had everything to keep me interested. It was made of dark wood like the bed and contained two mirrors and three drawers. The second mirror was my secret. I never looked at the dressing table unless I was alone so I thought no one else knew about it. You slid it out and bent it

back and there it was! A second mirror hiding the first! On the surface of the dressing table she kept glass bottles half full of perfume, china trays holding metal necklaces decorated with coloured glass beads. Everything to keep me happy. Then there were large windows with lace curtains, through which you could see the tennis courts across the road, behind a green chaise longue with a matching cylindrical cushion which I enjoyed lying on.

Around the corner there was a small table and a set of shelves accommodating brown-and-white photographs, small glass vases and china birds. Two large (dark wood) old-fashioned wardrobes, one for Grandma and one for Grandad, with metal handles, one slightly smaller than the other, took up the rest of the space back to the door.

I like their bungalow, although the only place where I can feel alone is on the gate into the front garden. It was about a year ago when Grandma became so ill that she had to go to a strange place for a test. When it was decided that she was not coming back, Grandad expressed a wish to acquire a cat. When he was a little boy in Wales they had always had a cat but he had not been able to cope with one with Grandma. Sadly we could only find a pair and at first he refused to take them. Eventually he took them in as it was them or nothing and he really wanted a cat to keep him company. Smudge ran away when he was quite new anyway and Squiggles sticks to Grandad like glue.

Around six months after she went into the Home we heard that Grandma was not eating. I couldn't bear it. I ran upstairs to my bedroom and Verity followed. She found me crying by my rocking-horse and I turned to her.

"You never knew, Verity. She was already bad when you were born."

She stood by helplessly, watching me cry, then left.

Amazingly, the expected did not happen and Grandma soon recovered. At the moment Mummy and Grandad go to see her often. She fell over about a month ago and hurt her head but of course I only know this from what Mummy has told me.

On 2nd March 2001, the day before my nanny's birthday, snow fell. I was so excited that as soon as I arrived home I ran out to it, without a coat or vest. I swirled in it and with it, like a snowflake myself I became part of the magical snow storm. Some things are good in life.

By Hannah Sherwin, aged 10
The Lady Eleanor Holles School, Hampton Hill

My Sister Nearly Died

My name is Kimberley and I'm nine years old. This is how I felt at the most difficult time of my life. My little sister's name is Chelsea. She is physically disabled and is epileptic. She can speak but not in full sentences. There are only several words she can say properly, the rest sound similar to when a very small child is speaking to you. She wears a calliper which is a metal thing that goes down her leg and has straps made out of leather and metal buckles. She wears special boots that her calliper can fix onto. This helps her to walk. She also wears a helmet to protect her head.

Chelsea is very special to me and is nice to play with. I do sometimes wonder what it's like to have a normal sister.

Chelsea was given lots of different medicines to make her better, but they did not work. We were told she needed a big operation where half of her brain would be taken out. It is called a hemispherectomy.

When she was taken into hospital I went and stayed with my grandad. He lived six hours away. I was only supposed to stay there for two weeks but I was there a bit longer. I felt really worried and scared and phoned Mum and Dad every day.

After two weeks I saw Chelsea in intensive care. She looked

terrible. Mum and Dad told me she needed sleep to get better. She had bandages all round her head. She had a respirator which helped her to breathe. She was on a drip. Chelsea had loads of other wires attached to her. It looked like the inside of a space ship.

After a while I went to stay with my nan. She was closer to the hospital than Grandad. At first I refused to go home, and stayed the night at the hospital with Chelsea, then I went back to Nan's. I went to see Chelsea nearly every day on the train. Chelsea woke up after four weeks. After she woke up Mum told me she hadn't been asleep but had been in a coma.

When Chelsea woke up after her operation I was really happy and couldn't wait until she came home. The doctors said she wouldn't be able to walk for eighteen months but she started walking after three months. Now she can walk, talk and has no fits. I am so much happier and I'm really proud of her for being so strong and staying alive while most would die. I really appreciate my sister. She's been through so much and I love her.

By Kimberley Greenaway, aged 9
St John's Primary School, Southport

The Night I Cut my Hair

Lots of little people do very silly things. I am going to tell you something silly I did.

I was in bed and I got up and went to the toilet and opened a drawer and found some scissors. I took them out, closed the door and crept to the mirror. I slowly opened the sharp points and SNIP SNIP, I had cut my hair!

I picked the hair up and put it in my toy box and put the scissors on the window ledge. I climbed back into bed and said to myself, "Shall I cut more hair off?" So I jumped out of bed, got the scissors off the window ledge, went to the mirror and SNIP SNIP, I had cut my hair again!

I looked at my reflection and I looked awful. So I put the scissors back in the bathroom, took the hair to my toy box, went to bed and fell fast asleep. I got up in the morning and went downstairs.

On the way downstairs I wondered if I would get shouted at. I slowly opened the door and Mum was not very happy; I could tell that by the look on her face.

She said, "Go and show Dad."

I was well scared but I went to show him and he said, "Stupid."

Mum shouted, "Hurry up, I'm taking you to the hairdressers."

So I went to the car and we drove down to Llani Barbers. When I was in the chair, the hairdresser said, "I have to do a number 1."

When she had finished I looked in the mirror and thought, "Everyone will laugh at me."

When I was in the car I wasn't very happy because I didn't want everyone to laugh at me. I pulled up to the school and took a big breath and started to walk to the door. I put my bag in the cloakroom, my mum kissed me goodbye and walked me to the hall door. I slowly opened the door and sat with my class.

I looked around the hall but no one was looking.

"Phew!" I thought. But I knew sooner or later people would laugh and I was right.

When I was on the bus going home the bus driver said, "What did you do to your hair?"

Everybody burst out laughing. When I was in bed I said, "I will never cut my hair again!"

By Joe Lewis-Clarke, aged 9
Llanidloes County Primary School, Llanidloes

My Holiday in Cornwall

In the summer holidays before I went into the Juniors me, Ste, Mum, Dad, Nana and Pop booked to go on a beautiful holiday in Cornwall.

First, we started packing, then jumped into the car and set off. The journey took seven hours to get to our holiday house! We went in my mum and dad's car and my nan and pop's car.

When we arrived there we started unpacking. I bet you would have loved to be there because it was OUTSTANDING! Later we sorted out who was going in which room. I had a little room but I had my mum and dad's room right next to me, and in that room there was a small short-cut to the kitchen. The house was old-fashioned and huge, it had many secret hiding places.

It was on a farm and we could see the white sheep. There was also a small games room outside.

Many times we went to Crackington Haven beach. It had hundreds of small rock pools and they were warm and the sea was cold and salty. The sea was surrounded by colossal cliffs. I used my bodyboard to surf on the big foamy waves. We went on long journeys on the cliffs. We saw wild ponies and quite a few blackberries. We visited a ruined ancient castle. And we saw a hovering bird of prey.

A couple of days later, we saw four runaway calves. They were really cute. Their mother was following them behind the fence and us and the calves were on the other side. We thought their mum was really angry because she kept mooing extremely loudly. But one of the calves started to go to its mummy and called the others. It took a long time but in the end they agreed.

Next day we had to get all the fun we could get. We bought me a toy and it was a Strike Force army truck. We also had a barbecue, the food was delicious. When it was time to go I was so tired I wanted my bed. We started packing and went home. I was allowed to have a Burger King on the way home. I was really disappointed because it was the best holiday I ever went on. I really hope I am allowed to go there again.

By Nathan Cowley, aged 8
St Margaret Mary's Junior School, Liverpool

Whale

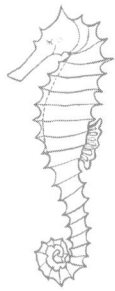

I was in South Africa and I was on my way to the beach. To get out of Cape Town, you had to go on the Mountain Road. The Mountain Road was a twisty, turning road that went round and round and round the mountain, spiralling into the sky. Of course, there were many mountain roads dotted around South Africa, but I hadn't quite realised that! Anyway, about the Mountain Road! It had crashing waves at the bottom, which slashed the crumbly rocks at the bottom of the mountain. I loved to watch the sea, trying to find a beach connected to it, way out beyond the horizon. Of course I never found such a place but it was just as entertaining to imagine.

As I looked out to sea I wondered what kind of sea creatures lived in it. Maybe brightly coloured corals, or maybe outstanding tropical fish with vivid colours just flashing out. Perhaps there were manatees waddling about on the sea-shore. It might have been possible there were sea-horses clinging onto seaweed as they swam, and that's another thing, maybe there were forests of kelp, like the ones in the Cape Town aquarium. There might have been dolphins, gracefully pushing through the water. But the most exciting thought of all was whales. Blue whales, spouting water, coming to the surface of the water and then plunging in again.Yes, seeing a blue whale would be brilliant. But it doesn't just work like that; you don't just decide you want to see a whale and just see it. Or do you?

Some time passed and I was still imagining corals and tropical fish and manatees and sea-horses and kelp, diving dolphins and blue whales. Then I saw it. A tiny dot, way out in the distance where my beach was supposed to be. I couldn't help noticing that something was shooting out of the dot. It vanished.

"No," I thought. "This can't be."

But then the thing appeared again! I could definitely tell that it was blue and water was coming out of it. It disappeared again but appeared even closer, then again and again and again. It now looked like a blue cucumber. It suddenly lurched forward really far and then I realised! A BLUE WHALE, I HAD SEEN IT!

Soon the car passed the whale, but I had such a clear image of him in my head that I saw him skimming the water and plunging down again, a great blue sausage in the water. Suddenly a road led off the mountain and we travelled beside the sea until we were at the beach. I searched the blue sea for him but he was gone. I couldn't help feeling upset.

But I could always imagine him.

Whale.

By Lauren Pigott, aged 9
Headington Junior School, Oxford

Winner, Year 4 ✳

Grandad's Day

My eyes snapped open as a shaft of sunlight pierced through my curtains. I was immediately awake. Today was Grandad's day.

Quickly the house was full of noise and bustle as we all struggled to get ready in time. Mummy seemed unusually stressed. Perhaps it was because it was Grandad's day.

As usual poor old Nicole, my younger sister, was taking the brunt of Mum's frustration. Somehow she always seems to wind her up.

Oliver, the baby of the family, was doing his best to get ready himself although he was only four. James, my older brother, was sailing through absent-mindedly as usual.

Finally, after what seemed an age, we all bundled into the Discovery.

All of a sudden we were off. Does Mum know the way? She still seems wound up from the rigours of getting us all ready, or maybe it was just because it was Grandad's day. It was still early in the morning and I was trying to get some sleep, but how could I with Nicole asking Mum and Dad continuously "Are we nearly there?" when we have just come out of our driveway. James and Oliver were quite happy playing Gameboy. It was just me that was bored and tired. Although I couldn't help thinking about what today was about.

Mum kept on telling me that today was Grandad's day, but what was this Grandad's day? And why was everyone looking sad and stressed? Soon I fell asleep.

Bleep!

I woke with a shock. Mum had just swerved past a car and turned sharply into a parking space. We had arrived at my nanny's house.

My brothers and sister and I all ran out of the car. The door was open so we all burst through the door joyfully and my sister even shouted "happy birthday". We ran into the living room where all nanny's relatives and friends were. Everyone was wearing black clothes and had sad faces. Where was Grandad? Something was wrong.

Nanny had just come downstairs crying. Was it because she was happy and Grandad was special or was it something else? I was confused. My brothers and my sister were playing with old toys and enjoying themselves, so I thought I would join them. There were wooden pieces shaped like egg timers and strips of string. You lie the strip of string on the floor, put the wooden piece shaped like an egg timer on the string, lift the string and do lots of tricks. It was really quite fun.

Suddenly two limos pulled up outside. It was the limo that was taking us to the party or wherever we were going. Everyone climbed in and the people who were left drove their own car.

We arrived and everyone slowly climbed out. There stood a church. Maybe it was their wedding day. But the church was dark and gloomy and everyone was wearing black clothes. It couldn't be. Suddenly a horse and cart passed and it was carrying a coffin, and on top were flowers bunched together and in the centre it said the word "Grandad". As soon as it passed us everyone burst out crying. I was sure in that coffin was my Grandad and now I knew why everyone was so upset.

We entered the church and sat down on the bench. The service began. I was so upset; I was probably the loudest one crying in the whole church. We all had to sing lots of songs and say lots of prayers but the worst part of the service was when he was taken away in his coffin and burnt; his cremation. I couldn't bear to watch it so I ran out of the hall and sat outside by the flowers. Soon the service was over, we were shown around the gardens and then we drove back to my great-aunt's house.

We stepped in the door and saw a table full of food like sausage rolls, crisps, mini sausages, cup cakes and a large salmon in the centre. This was the largest salmon I had ever seen and it was bright pink and around the plate were cucumber, tomatoes and lettuce. Everyone started eating straight away and talking. Once everyone had a drink they became more relaxed and it started to get noisy and feel like a party.

I went upstairs to the loo but realised it was locked and that an old man was stuck in there; he couldn't open the door. I ran downstairs to get Mum and as soon as she went upstairs everyone followed. Seeing we couldn't open the door from the outside, my step-brother Silas had to climb out the window, onto the roof to collect the man.

It was getting late, the younger ones had fallen asleep and Mum decided that it was time to go home, so we said goodbye to everyone and boarded the Discovery. We were all very tired and cold. Mummy and Daddy were a little drunk and they had the music on loud so everyone was getting a headache. I was hoping we didn't lose track of where we were going.

James and I were talking about what had happened but it

was difficult to hear ourselves speak with all that music on. Later on the music wasn't so loud and James and I went to sleep. I had a dream that we were on holiday in Barbados staying in a beautiful villa. We were with my mum's mum, and my dad's mum and dad, the sun was shining and Grandad and I were playing in the swimming pool when he needed some sun cream on so he went inside to put some on and when he came back out he saw that my armbands had fallen off and that I was drowning so he dived into the pool and saved me. He was my hero.

I woke up and found myself lying in bed. I wasn't sure whether Grandad was still alive or not. I went to ask Mum and she said that he was dead; I remembered about Grandad saving me and was very upset, I didn't think he deserved to die.

Even though Grandad was dead I could still picture him in my head and whenever I went anywhere it felt like he was still there beside me always. I will never forget him.

"I love you Grandad."

By Emma Bartlett, aged 10
The Lady Eleanor Holles School, Hampton Hill

Friendship Tie

Me and my friend have been having large fights lately, that's the problem. It was a bright and sunny day in May, while I wondered whether it was going to be outdoor lunch. Finally, the teacher came in from the office. She told our class that a new girl was coming. I quickly budged up one seat so that that was the only space in class. I watched the door carefully.

It was pushed open by our headmaster Mr Powell; he has grey hair and he is funny with a warm smile. He was followed by a lady with wild brown hair. With her she pushed a boy in a pushchair, with the same styled hair as the mother, but it was blond. They were followed by a tall girl of about my age, with blue eyes and long blonde, frizzy hair. She stood shyly behind her mother, peeping out at times.

The teacher explained the rules of the game the class was playing although she did at last usher her to the seat beside mine. I looked at her and said cheerfully, "Hi!" The girl smiled but she looked very empty. I could hear her feet clicking under the table and I could tell that she was nervous, because I click my feet when I get nervous too! I stifled a giggle as I remembered what the girl had looked like. She had peeped out so many times that she had looked like a jack-in-the-box! I took my eyes

over to where the teacher was standing. She winked at me so I said quickly, "Right, uh, well, what's your name?"

"Katie," the girl said timidly.

"Good, now we can begin!" I grinned and we started the game.

The game was a little bit like Battleships, but I can't remember the exact details. Anyway, to cut a long story short I won the first game and Katie won the second. I guess this was lucky because Katie might have got upset otherwise. I remember that Katie had spoken to the other Katie and apparently they had a lot in common! I said, "Do you want to play with us outside?"

"No, I'm playing with the other Katie!"

The day seemed a battle to win Katie's friendship. But alas! I didn't.

The next day was poetry day in our class. Each of us read a poem out of our poetry books. Katie didn't have a poem because all her poem books were still packed in their boxes! I saw her by the poetry display. Her clog was beside all this (Katie had come from a school in Holland). It had been signed by all her old best friends. I walked up to her but she sidled away.

I sat with my best friend Livvy on a log in the back playground while we ate our lunch. We had decided to give up. Katie was obviously best friends with Katie F. Me and Livvy sat in silence all through lunch. Questions were swimming in my head. Why Katie F? She's pretty boring anyway! Then I looked at myself in the cloakroom mirror. I wondered aloud, "What am I saying? It's Katie's choice who she picks as a best friend."

Once Livvy had finished her lunch we sat swinging on the greenhouse. "Do you still want to be my friend?" a small voice said. It was Katie. I could see she had gone bright red!

"Sure!" I replied. And that was the day we became three.

By Abigail Waite, aged 8
Burton Bradstock School, Burton Bradstock

Gerbils

Mum and Dad were sitting at the table after breakfast when I thought that, now Dad was there, I just ought to spit it out, or I wouldn't get the gerbils I'd set my heart on. So I leant forward and asked, "Mum, please can you coax Dad to get me the hamster and gerbils this half-term?"

Mum sighed, "I will."

Full of satisfaction and suspense, I bounded up the stairs and curled like a hedgehog on the top step – or rather the second one down – and tried to shut my ears to the voices coming from the kitchen.

After about six minutes, I jumped down half the stairs, jumped down the second half to the last step, ran into the long room like a hare and yelled, "MUM HAVE YOU FINISHED YET?"

Mum answered, "No!"

So I scooted off to the downstairs bathroom, locked the door, sat on the toilet, picked up a book and tried to get some sense out of several long poems, and about a quarter of an hour later walked into the kitchen.

"Well," I said, "have you coaxed him?"

Mum smiled. "This half-term," said she, "we are going to get your gerbils and Ben's hamster. But ask Daddy, he's the expert."

"Dad," I asked him, "can we really get them?"

Dad's eyes closed momentarily. "Well, it seems that it's too late to say no."

I was slightly disappointed when we entered the shop. It was quite small, was full of things for animals and had hardly any people in it.

There might, of course, be some animals in it. I paced around the shop, picking out bowls, staring at water bottles that would never fit my gerbils, and seeing, with Ben, if there were any rabbit collars. We found some beautiful tropical fish, but no hamsters!

Mum was the one that found Scampy. There were several cages on top of each other. On one of them was stuck a label that said "Syrian Hamster". Nothing was visible except some straw and food though. So Mum alerted the lady of the shop and she took out a small, sleeping bundle. As she explained about it, I couldn't help looking at Ben's happy, happy face.

I stared into the box. In it were about fifty gerbils. Running, playing, peeping out of houses. The two males I liked best were a fawn one, with pinkish eyes, and a black one, with a white bit.

A few minutes later, sitting in the car, I hugged the boxes on my knee and thought gladly about the phrase on them: "Your new pet is enclosed".

Your new Pet is enclos

By Beth Jellicoe, aged 8
Ruckleigh School, Solihull

51

My Unbearable Burn

This outstandingly horrible thing happened to me when I was about six or seven years old. I had broken up for the summer holidays and I travelled home in a car with my grandmother and grandad. When we got home, Grandmother chose to start cooking dinner early. The cooker is rather annoying at times, for there is an uneasy prop that is rather wobbly, that you have to put your pans on. I came into the kitchen and as I was getting near the pan containing heated olive oil, it slipped and it just caught the side of my arm.

I drew back with astonishment. My arm hurt so badly! Grandad put it under cold water and bandaged it up. No one could have known how painful it was. It was aching badly and it had gone purple and red. The stings were still there from the vicious thrashes of the oil as it spilt.

When my parents came back, my dad was rather upset. He took me for a little walk and told me about what had happened to him when he was a little boy. My mum got me an appointment at the hospital. I had never been there before. I felt quite uneasy and scared. I had to wait a long time before it was my turn because there was a boy before me with a burn down his face.

I started to feel I was really lucky. I would never experience what he had to experience. It would be nice if all the people who had burns like that could be saved from losing some of their most valuable abilities, but they can't. When I took the bandages off, it was all red and flaky. I was even told that I would probably have a scar for the rest of my life. I would like to help children like me but worse, children who have burns on their faces because, I must say, it is a nasty experience.

By Alice Seville, aged 8
Prep Dept, Edgbaston High School, Birmingham

Selling my Grandmother's House

Some of the happiest days were spent at The Shrubbery, my grandmother's house for forty years. She lived two and a half hours from London in a small coastal village on the Essex marshland.

We travelled late at night, in order not to waste the day, and, so that I could pop straight into bed when I arrived without having to unpack my suitcase, I always wore my soft, striped pyjamas and my woolly dressing gown and slippers. I was allowed a pillow and a travel rug in the car and I used to nurse my two teddies on my lap. I loved the darkness and the rain splattering on the windscreen and the regular beat of the wipers. Sometimes I would pretend I was an intrepid explorer lost at sea.

The most wonderful thing about Granny's house was that nothing ever changed. The entrance to the garden was through an arched latched gate, over which a thick hedge had grown and, in springtime, the hedge often hid blackbirds' nests. Sometimes, when I passed through the gate, I felt like the mole from 'The Wind in the Willows' visiting his old home. Granny would be sitting in the armchair by the bay window, watching for our car. It was my job to stand opposite the security light, to keep it on, so we could see where we were walking. When the light first shone, I would often catch glimpses of hedgehogs and foxes' tails, disappearing into the bushes.

We walked into a warm, cosy kitchen with Granny waiting for us, her arms open wide ready to hug us. The dining room table was set with plates of sandwiches, biscuits and slices of homemade fruitcake. The napkins were of starched linen, neatly folded and placed on fine bone china tea plates. Tea was poured from her old silver teapot, which stood next to a taller, silver hot water jug. I used to think they were husband and wife standing together with their two children – the milk jug and sugar basin.

In the winter, Granny would have a fire lit in the sitting room and I would snuggle up in there against Granny's bony knees, listening to the sea wind howling to be let free. In the mornings, I was woken by the cooing of a pigeon, which used to perch on the chimney above my room. I always ate breakfast at a small table by the window, so I could throw bacon rinds to the seagulls and watch them circle and swoop down to catch them. Next I would make an inspection of all the rooms to make sure nothing had changed. My favourite room was the box room in which the old treadle sewing machine stood, its drawers full of old hat pins, shoe horns and darning mushrooms. The bottom drawer was the most exciting of all, full to the top with every sort of button you could imagine. I used to sit in the rocking-chair, my feet buried in the sheepskin rug, sorting out my favourites.

The garden was full of fruit trees and the kitchen cupboards were stacked with plum jam. There was always a musty smell in the sheds from the old apple racks. My grandfather's workshop still smelt of paint, even though he had died several years ago. My grandfather was a sea captain and very ordered in his ways. Everything was exactly how he left it, with all the nails and screws in labelled jars, his tools oiled and hung on hooks, except a small saw which lay on the workbench. I often wondered what he had been making just before he died. The drawers were lined with newspaper dated 1963, browned with age but perfectly flat.

Grandpa had made my brothers a tree house in the old walnut tree. It wasn't very high and had the vegetable patch below it, so that we had a soft landing if we fell. I had been too young to use it while he was alive but it was where I used to

think, when I grew bigger. When I heard that Granny was going to sell The Shrubbery, I was in despair and climbed into the tree house to consider what my parents had said.

Selling the house and buying a flat, which would be easier for Granny to manage, was the practical solution, but I felt sick whenever I thought about it. It was true – Granny had become frail and forgetful and she was finding the house and garden a worry. Granny was not like she used to be. She seemed to be shrinking faster than the jam in the jars in the cupboard. Meals took for ever and my brothers laughed and said she was chewing for Britain. An electric fire was moved into the sitting room and we started eating take-away on the car journey so she didn't have to cook for us when we arrived. Moss had grown over the paths and the climbers concealed the windows, ivy covered the birdbath and the apple picker had blown over and broken.

The 'For Sale' board was nailed onto the wooden fence. Granny was upset because the agent split the wood in his hurry. I hated the people who bought the house, especially the children, who slid down the banisters and kicked their football into the flowerbeds. The new owners divided the garden and built two ugly bungalows in it. We seldom visit Granny. She comes to us in a taxi.

In Granny's house there used to be a big, fat Buddha with a golden tummy. My granny had brought him back from India. We always rubbed his tummy for good luck and made a wish. He is in our sitting room now. I don't think his magic works any more and I'll never understand why we sold my granny's home.

By Lydia Mavridoglou, aged 11
Wimbledon High Junior School, London

Joint Winner, Year 6

Wobbly Tooth

Two weeks ago my white tooth came out. I was very excited. At school my mum was trying to twist it. I couldn't eat a thing.

When I got home from school, Sam's friend was at the dinner table ready for tea. Then, five minutes later, Sam came in for tea and all the rest of the people. I sat at the table quietly, my tooth was as wobbly as a bowl of jelly. I would not eat any tea because of my tooth; it was hurting so much. It had lost two strings.

My mum pulled it and twisted it and all of a sudden my white tooth popped out. It was bleeding for half an hour.

That night I put my tooth under my pillow and in the morning my tooth was gone! I ran to show my mum my two pounds I got from the tooth fairy. I could go and spend it now but I didn't. I wanted to save up all my money.

I saw some fairy dust on my pillow. I used it to make my toys a pretty dress. And whenever I look at the dress it reminds me of when my white milk tooth came out.

By Beth Riordan, aged 7
Tutshill Primary School, Chepstow

The Trenches in Italy

We've been to Italy twice. Both times we stayed for a couple of days in the mountains. We were discussing where we should go, what we should do, when a friend mentioned some World War I trenches. This shot up to the top of the list; before we knew it, we were on our way.

The trenches were positioned at the top of the mountain, and a great big spiral road twisted up to them. Once we got to the top, we sat down for a bit, merely to catch our breath. Although the sun was scorching in the sky, and we were only in T-shirts and shorts, I sensed a cold black mist of terror in the air. Despite this, I ran on, eager to walk in soldiers' footsteps.

As I entered the first tunnel, the daylight seemed to disappear behind me. I guided myself by keeping close to the cold, damp wall. Every now and again, a slit of sunlight would project onto the side of a tunnel, but only when I passed a window. Actually, this was more of a hole, just big enough for a gun to sneak through.

This underground city seemed so deathly silent, so calm. I imagined it during the war, bustling with soldiers, queuing up to die. Bullet-holes would have decorated those dull, grey walls. An abandoned pack of rations lay in the corner, rotting. This was over half a century ago, yet somehow I could still feel the horror of it all.

Soon, I came to some stone stairs, leading back up to the world of light and warmth. I took a deep breath of fresh air, since the trenches were so closed up. Was it my imagination, or did I really smell gunpowder? Regardless, I walked on, gaping at the enormous amount of openings in the ground, leading to darkened passages of sorrow. One was slightly away from the others and had a larger entrance cave. As I edged further into it, I noticed it had a narrow staircase going deeper underground. This was lit by dim, flickering torches, and smelt like the sewers.

Several paths led out from here, but I chose the one which was, or seemed, the longest. Small chambers parted off in all directions; I glanced at them, but carried on walking straight. When I came out, I was face to face with a graveyard. Monuments lay crooked in the turf, and were all dedicated to those who had died fighting for their country. A huge iron gate was slightly ajar, so I stepped in. Vast granite gravestones contrasted with smaller, marble ones. Hundreds of names, printed in this small garden, lurking out at me.

Could've sworn. Could've sworn I saw him. Just for a split second … a soldier.

Dominik Bienkowski, aged 10
Shoreside Primary School, Ainsdale

Lost on the Lilo

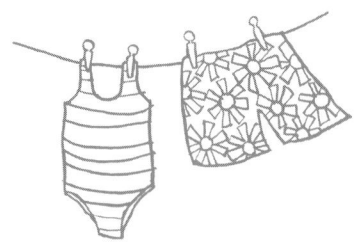

CRASH! SPLASH! WHOOSH!

Wow! The waves are very big today. It's nearly always sunny in Morocco, but the sea isn't always calm. I love coming to Morocco because I can enjoy the sun and the beach, and this year my Moroccan grandparents had rented a house which was practically on the beach, so all you had to do was walk out the front door and the beach was in front of you.

It's not only the weather and the beach I like about Morocco, but I also like to see my Moroccan family there. Usually I don't see all my family because there's so many! So I have to travel to different parts of Morocco and nearly every year I meet five or six new relatives, and I'm pretty sure I haven't met all of them yet.

But one of my favourite ones, that I see every year, is called Driss. He's my best friend when I go to Morocco and he's also my cousin. We have lots of fun together swimming in the sea and playing in the sand; we also have lots of adventures together. But I didn't know the biggest one yet was still to come.

When the waves calmed down a bit I went over to his house (me and Driss live in separate houses, which is just as well because sometimes we argue a lot) and I asked him if he would like to come on the lilo with me. He was having lunch so he said, in Arabic of course, "I'll be there in 15 minutes." "OK," I replied (again in Arabic).

At the beach, I waited HALF an HOUR and finally Driss' head came into view. The rest of the family were all under the parasol so I took the lilo from the house myself, got changed into my swimming costume and set off for the sea. Me and Driss both lay down on the lilo and just relaxed. We didn't realise the waves were getting stronger, we didn't realise we were getting further and further away from our family, our house, the beach.

We didn't realise any of this until I got water splashed in my face. I sat up to wipe my eyes and I saw what looked like a long yellow sheet far away with tiny ants crawling on it. Driss was sitting up now and he looked worried. I certainly was. What were we going to do? We were so far away. Suddenly I saw a dark, black shadow in the water, and I thought it was a sting-ray!

"Aaaagh!" I cried.

"What?" said Driss calmly.

"Look!" I said, and pointed to the black shadow.

"It's only a harmless plastic bag," he said, and he fished out a broken, black plastic bag.

"Oh," I said, blushing.

First we tried to paddle with our hands, but the waves were too strong and we didn't get anywhere. I tried to stand up and call for help, but I couldn't even see my family and even if I could they wouldn't hear me. I tried to act cool, but inside I started to get panicky.

In the end we decided to take turns getting into the water and pushing the lilo. I went first and when I was pushing the lilo I really did see a large fish under me! I jumped onto the lilo saying it was Driss' turn, because I didn't want to confess I was scared of a large fish.

"But you've only had two minutes!" Driss said, and then we got into an argument about how long we would have each. In the end he tipped the lilo over and I was thrown into the water.

I came out spluttering, and I was prepared to push him back, but I decided not to start up a fight in the sea, out of my depth (far out of my depth) because when he was angry he was not very nice! I knew that because two or three years ago, he had tried to duck me! So I just carried on with my go, trying to ignore the fish under me, but I still felt a bit scared and angry with Driss for pushing me.

We carried on taking turns to push until we could see our family. I felt really pleased but tried not to show it. When we pushed the lilo on the beach I was about to jump up and clap hands with Driss, but then I remembered I was waiting for him to say sorry first.

That evening he still hadn't said sorry and he still wasn't talking to me. And because it was my last day and I didn't want to leave with us still being angry with each other, I went to say sorry (even though I didn't do anything) and give him a present (money) because it was our last day. So I said sorry and he said sorry and we were friends again.

"I must give you something!" Driss suddenly said.

"You don't have to," I said, for I knew he was quite poor. But he went into his house and came out with a small white container. I opened it, and inside were the smallest shells I'd ever seen, smaller than a quarter of your small fingernail.

"It's not much," he said.

"But I still love them!" I replied.

And it was true.

By Sara Charteris-Black, aged 9
Sandfield County Primary School, Guildford

A Moving Experience

My nanny was brilliant. In my eyes she was a loving and caring person. Nanny was very fashion conscious and adored shopping. She was a great and super Nan.

Sadly, seven months ago my nanny died. It was an emotional experience for me. I was distraught by the loss and traumatically upset. Unfortunately I was not the only person to suffer. My mum, too, took it very badly because Nanny meant a lot to her and they had a very strong mother – daughter relationship. Also, Mum was the person who found Nanny sitting on the lavatory and Mag talking to her softly saying "hurry up and wake up".

Before Nanny died in the morning, she had got all the breakfast things out and ready. As Nanny and Mag like a cup of coffee in the morning for breakfast, she had put the kettle on the gas cooker and while the kettle was boiling she went to the toilet. Sadly that is where she died.

It was good thinking of Mum's to go to Nanny's flat because every morning Mum used to do a security check, by telephoning with her good morning call. Unfortunately this time Nanny didn't answer. Mag had always shut doors behind her, which probably saved her life, because when Mum broke into the flat the kitchen was filled with hazed smoke.

Of course there were all my nanny's friends to consider and lots, lots more. It was quite sad telling all Nanny's friends that she had died. Unfortunately Nanny had to have an autopsy. Eventually the autopsy was over. I do not really know what Nanny died of.

The one person that I really felt sorry for was my Auntie Margaret. Margaret has a disability called 'Down's Syndrome' which means she has limited understanding. Mag, we call her for short, is my mum's twin sister. Lots of people wouldn't think so because they do not look alike. Mag is a loving and kind person. She is forty-four years old but she only has a mentality of a three or four year-old.

Mag is like a little sister to me. Mag has a wonderful personality. If I could choose a colour for her it would be peach because it is soft and fluffy and that is what Mag is inside her heart. Sometimes Mag is a bit of a pain because she has mood swings. However, most of the time she's happy and full of laughter.

Two weeks after Nanny's death it was her funeral. On the day of Nanny's funeral we had to go into Nanny's old flat. We waited for the special car to take us to the church but Mag wouldn't go in the flat. She never entered the flat after Nanny died. So Mum had to take her to Ann's (a neighbour over the road). When the car arrived I had to run over the road and get Mag.

Mag went in the car but wasn't very co-operative. She had a strong sense of what was going on. In her own way she knew she was saying a loving goodbye to her mum. When the funeral period was over it was time for Mag to move in with Mum, Dad and I. For a couple of nights Mag slept in the spare room, with my mum on the floor to get Maggie used to her new home. About a week later my dad got a white van from work so we could transfer all Mag's belongings. Unfortunately the van could only fit three people so Mum had to stay at home while Dad, Mag and I drove to Nanny's old neighbour named Ann, because we had to drop Mag off.

I was not as strong as Dad, so we had to go back for Mum. It took at least one week for Mum to sort everything out, but all her hard work paid off. It was easy to stack the van. It was sad at the same time because there was over fifty years of life and history. Mum got a bit upset because most of her life was spent there and it was very close to her heart. When we got home Mum, Dad and I unloaded everything from the van. After we finished fitting all Mag's belongings in her room, we went back to collect her from Ann. We were very grateful to Ann. She said, "It was no problem."

Mag was excited and delighted to see all her things in her new room. Mag placed everything in her room as it was in her old room. She was a bit upset at the same time. The one thing that she noticed straight away was the size of her room, because it was smaller. The main problem was that Nanny's flat was on the ground floor but our house has two floors so Mag had to climb the stairs. First of all we thought that the stairs would be a bit of an obstacle course for Mag; however, she managed it very well, but at a speed of a snail. Mag loved tissues, papers and magazines so she would nick things from Mum and race up the stairs to hide them before Mum could catch her.

A few days later Mum contacted Mag's special day centre, which she attends weekly from Monday to Friday. She is very familiar with its colourful surroundings and its lively atmosphere. Mum felt that if Mag spent time with her friends it would provide her with the security, support and friendship which she needed at this sad time.

Mag now lives a happy life again, hopefully! We all love her although her fingers have a habit of going into OTHER people's chests of drawers! AHHHHHH!

By Sabina McCann, aged 11
St John Fisher Primary School, Perivale

When the Finger Met the Door

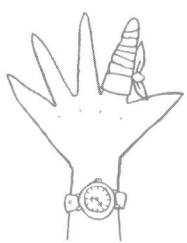

It was a bright, sunny afternoon and I was very hot. I was at school and all the windows in the classroom were open. We were finishing off, so everyone was doing something different. I was making the bookshelves tidy. I finished, so I thought I would go and draw a picture. I found my pencil but I saw that it was blunt. I wandered over to the bin and picked up a sharpener. I sharpened my pencil and set off back to my seat.

Just as I was on my way back, something terrible happened. I put my hand on the door of the quiet room and someone from the inside opened it. My hand slipped and my middle finger fell into the hinge. The door closed and my finger was still trapped. It was agony! At first I thought I would be able to get it out but I couldn't.

I started to scream, "AAGH! HELP!"

Everyone in the room looked around at me. I couldn't believe what was happening. Mrs Chubb called an ambulance. Then she phoned my mum and she got to the school really quickly. They wrapped my finger up in a bandage and soon the ambulance was there. The ambulance man picked me up and carried me away. We got to the ambulance and my class was there waving. My finger was really hurting now. I could feel blood on my hand. My finger had come off. They put me on a bed in the ambulance and sped away.

They drove on for quite a while. Eventually we reached Western Hospital. I was put on a stretcher and carried inside. Then I got lifted onto a bed and a nurse and doctor came over. Mum was crying. My bandage got taken off and I very quickly closed my eyes. It was disgusting. The doctor had a good look and said, "No doctor in this hospital is clever enough to sew this finger back on. You will have to go to Bristol. Sorry." This was bad.

We got back into the ambulance and set off. In no time at all we were at Frenchey Hospital in Bristol. A nurse came out to help Mum carry me in. They put me on a bed and in about one hour I was having my operation. It was weird. They gave me an injection so I soon fell asleep. It took them about two hours to get it sewn back on again. When I woke up I was back on my hospital bed, my finger all bandaged up.

Next day I was able to go home. I got loads of presents and cards. I couldn't use my hand for ages because it was in a sling. In the end I got used to it and now it's healed very well.

By Molly Huxtable, aged 9
Wedmore First School, Wedmore

Alex

Alex. That name seems like a huge lump of sadness now.

Have you ever wished that you could live one part of your life over? I wish that every time I think of the name Alex. Alex is, or was, my absolute, top of the charts, number one best friend. I met him when I was very young – one year old, in fact. My family had just moved to Singapore from Australia. He was one year older than me, but by the time we could talk, we were the best of friends. His mother ran a play school at her house, and when I was old enough, I attended it.

It was a big house with a long driveway, which led to a small patch of asphalt. The asphalt was shaded by an overhang of the house. On the asphalt, play toys would be scattered. There were some steps that led to a porch where there was a corner where you could dress up and play 'house'. Also, there was a blue plastic tarp filled with water where the class would perform 'experiments'. The porch led to two glass doors.

The first one led to a dining room. It was a rather large room with a wooden table on the right which had a sheet of glass in the middle of it. To the left of the room there was a lounge in which there was an assortment of nice sofas and a small wooden table. The children in the play school were never allowed in the dining room or the lounge unless they were on their way to the kitchen. The second door led to the classroom. It was split into two sections: the class section where all the kids worked on projects on little red tables, and the library section in which we stored all the books.

Sometimes Alex would come home from his school, Tanglin, and would come in and greet his mother, so I would see him. I can't remember Alex's face clearly any more, but from what I can remember, he had golden brown hair and light hazel eyes with tanned skin. He always seemed to have a smile on his face and an adventure in mind.

Once he tried to catch some pigeons on his driveway, although they flew away as he came near. Another time, he nailed some wooden planks to a tree and climbed up. The tree was about six feet high. It had two forks, a short one and a long one. Up the long tree fork, Alex told me that there was a wasps' nest, so he did not put any steps up there. I chickened out of both these things, but he laughed good-naturedly.

You know how I was saying I wished I could live a period of my life again? These were the years I would have lived over. I WOULD have chased the pigeons; I WOULD have climbed the tree. Sadly, not many of my wishes come true. After five years of living in Singapore and five years of a great friendship, my father had to change jobs and move to a different country. Don't ask me why; he never explained it to me. My dad had to move to Poland.

At first, my sister and I were really excited. We ordered winter clothes from the magazine 'Landsend' and spent hours in front of the mirror trying them on. Then I began to realise what this meant. No Alex, and no way of contacting him apart from the telephone (I hadn't heard of e-mail then). I began to worry.

I was very scared when Mrs Tillis drove my family to the airport. We had an okay time leaving. Alex and I got a picture together, and we fooled around. When I was on the plane, I cried in the toilet so no one would see. When we got to Poland, Mrs Tillis called us and told my mum how Alex had cried all the way back to their house. I kept in contact with Alex, but it was less and less frequent.

After two years in Poland, my dad transferred to England. We had barely been there for a month, when my mum told me the news. Alex had leukaemia. When they told me I said, "Oh", as if I knew what it meant. The truth is I didn't. In the Christmas break, my family went to Singapore for a vacation. When I saw Alex I was horrified. Instead of having his usual mat of golden brown hair, he was practically bald and instead of being cheerful, he was harsh to everyone except my mum and me!

I whispered fiercely to my mother, "What happened to him!"

"He might die, James. That's what leukaemia does. This is just a sign that he has leukaemia."

I was fuming with rage. Thoughts were racing through my head. Why hadn't she told me? Why was Alex like this? Will he survive? Yes, he just HAS to survive. He HAS to, I mean, this is Alex I'm talking about, right?

After a little while, I started calming down. It wasn't my mother's fault Alex was like this. Anyway, how was she meant to know I didn't know what leukaemia meant. I acted as if I knew. I started blaming myself. I should have worried more, cared more but, NO, I had to play Mr Big Jerk and go on with regular life, caring about how much money I had to save to buy a new computer game and when the baseball season began.

I was a jerk, a big jerk. I hated myself.

After I got over the shock of seeing Alex this way, I started having fun with him, playing a new computer game called 'Carmen Sandiego JR'.

After that holiday, I had the same amount of fun as I had had before. I did start being less good at my schoolwork, but I was happy. I mean it was Alex. He could get through anything. Oh, how wrong I was.

It was a month before December, and I was playing my Playstation, when my mother called me down into the living room. I sat down on the couch thinking how boring this was, wishing I could get back to my game.

My mother told me what had happened. It came to me in a shock, a rush. Alex was dead. I lay on the couch, stunned, winded, devastated. Just imagine your number one, absolute top of the charts best friend DEAD. I couldn't believe it; I wouldn't believe it. I ran upstairs to my room, flung myself onto my bed and cried. I felt like I felt on that holiday in Singapore. I also felt ashamed. I hadn't worried one little bit about Alex. What type of friend was I? I just wished it had been me and not him, so he could have enjoyed just one more Christmas.

My family and I went to his funeral. I was the only kid who cried. Even his brother didn't cry.

I now know I could not have prevented Alex's death. I only hope God gave Alex a good place in the sky.

By James Ross, aged 10
The American School in England, Thorpe

Grandad

The wood-burning stove was always alight in my gran and grandad's house. Opening the sitting room door I would be met by the sweet smell of wood smoke mingled with the strong exotic aroma of Havana cigars. We all used to sit there after supper, perhaps of salmon steaks, green beans and roast potatoes, followed by my gran's homemade apple tart. I would sit with my cousins, my aunt and uncle and Gran and Grandad, crouching on the furry white rug in front of the stove, whilst Mum and Dad put my three younger brothers to bed upstairs.

I can see my grandad now in my mind's eye, puffing on a long cigar, his pipe and open book laying next to him, whilst Gran read the church magazine. From time to time my grandad would get up and poke the stove and put on a few more logs. All around the room, about ten centimetres below the ceiling, was a ledge displaying my gran's enormous collection of Beatrix Potter figures.

At last Mum and Dad would come down and then came the 'treat'. We all moved on to the 'best' sitting room, the room we children were never allowed in on our own.

Of course my brothers and I often crept into that room secretly, and I looked at all the strange objects there: the stuffed kingfisher in a glass case, the blue-and-white china, the creaky leather chairs. We were intrigued by the vast array of old photographs of family members long dead who we had heard of but never met. We would roll on the fluffy rugs and dare each other to touch and open the cedar cigar boxes.

There was such a vast array of books of all types. My grandad read all the time, not just one kind of book – he read everything. There was a whole shelf holding the complete works of Charles Dickens, a vast Times Atlas Of The Second World War, a Welsh dictionary. My brothers used to like to press the buttons on a shiny CD player, the front of which whizzed in and out automatically if lightly touched. We used to sit there guiltily pressing the buttons and watching the front of the machine glide in and out, in and out, until a cross parent discovered us and dragged us out.

There seemed to be so many things that we weren't allowed to do at my gran's. Why couldn't we go into that room? Why couldn't we stand on the stairs and swing the chandelier in the galleried landing? That used to drive my grandad wild. Why were we never given tea in the willow-patterned cups and saucers like the adults? It all seemed so unfair.

My grandad died suddenly on my brother's birthday. We went straight down to see Gran. Strangely the house seemed just the same, the ashtrays were full of cigar ash, the half-read books lay around.

The next time we visited Gran she was selling the old house. She had bought a flat in Harrogate to be near my aunt and uncle. This time the wood-burning stove was cold and dead, and the smell of tobacco only faintly perceptible. No half-full ashtrays, no half-read books. We still had quite a nice supper, but the atmosphere was different, and the tart had been bought, not homemade.

Gran didn't care any more about us going into the 'best' sitting room. As I reached towards the door handle I almost wanted to hear Gran's familiar voice behind me, "Not in there dear." But nobody came. I opened the door and switched on the light. The room looked cold, unused and unwelcoming. It had no air of excitement and I had no urge to explore further. Everything looked so dead. Even the stuffed kingfisher that had once seemed so lifelike looked dead. I shut the door quickly. What had happened to the world I had once known? I looked up and saw one of my brothers happily swinging the chandelier round and round. I rushed up to him and dragged him away from it.

How dare he do that? How dare he? And it was then that I realised, and understood, why I had not been allowed to do such things. My grandad had his own way of doing things and he didn't want it wrecked by unruly children. But now we missed him, his disapproval. It was part of our lives.

When I saw Gran's house for the last time I stood looking up at it in the pouring rain, memories flooding into my head. Going to Gran's would never be the same again.

I don't ever want to go back there, because in my mind the house will always belong to my gran and grandad, and I want those memories to live on for ever.

By Mary Matthias, aged 11
South Hampstead Junior High School for Girls, London

Joint Winner, Year 6 ✳

Some More Anthologies of Children's Writing

If you have enjoyed *Tell You What!* why not read the other anthologies of children's writing published by Cambridge University Press:

I'm Telling You!

The winning stories from the 1999 Cambridge Young Writers Award, featuring such pieces as 'Mr Quine Dissects the Owl', 'The Day I Walked in Wet Cement' and 'Owen's Calamity'. This collection of stories, written by children and reflecting their everyday lives, offers a fresh and compelling child's-eye view of life in today's complex world. Here are some of our writers of the future – their funny, poignant, sometimes tragic tales will stay with you for ever.

ISBN 0-521-78578-2

Write Here, Write Now:
A Celebration of Children's Writing

In March 2000, the Department for Education and Employment launched a new national writing competition for schools divided into four categories: story, poem, play script and film/TV script, each started off by a famous author and then completed by the children. *Write Here, Write Now: A Celebration of Children's Writing* is a fabulous collection of the winning entries in each genre; well crafted, imaginative, powerful, these pieces by talented young writers are wonderfully varied but each has some special quality which made it a winner and earned it a place in this book.

ISBN 0-521-79963-5

Write Here, Write Now 2001:
A Brilliant Collection of Children's Writing

For the 2001 'Write Here, Write Now' competition, the categories were story, poem, script and non-fiction. Four professional writers, Jacqueline Wilson (the novelist), John Hegley (the poet), Phil Redmond (the scriptwriter) and Tony Robinson (the writer, actor and presenter), each wrote the start of a piece for the children to build on. And what imaginative and high-quality writing emerged and is contained in this book of the winning entries! The pieces chosen by the judges are an uplifting testament to the creative talent of today's children.

ISBN 0-521-00885-9 (Publication date: November 2001)